T0113688

I Dare You to Love Yourself More

A GUIDE TO SELF-LOVE AND POSITIVE AFFIRMATIONS

DANA MARIE WILLIAMS

authorHOUSE®

AuthorHouse™
1663 Liberty Drive
Bloomington, IN 47403
www.authorhouse.com
Phone: 833-262-8899

Published by AuthorHouse 11/29/2021

ISBN: 978-1-6655-4530-3 (sc)
ISBN: 978-1-6655-4529-7 (e)

Library of Congress Control Number: 2021923872

Print information available on the last page.

This book is printed on acid-free paper.

Dedication

I dedicate this book to my mother, Vera, and my father, Ernest. Your sacrifices were not in vain. You cultivated and nurtured my spirit and heart so that I can achieve mountains with you by my side and every step of the way. I will be forever grateful for extraordinary parents like you.

In addition, I dedicate this book to my close friends for always pouring genuine love and support into my adventurous ideas and spirit. I love you all.

A few simple tips for life: feet on the ground,
head to the skies, heart open … quiet mind.
—Buddha

Quote from the author

You have a purpose in this Universe. Your energy, joy and light is uniquely made for you to serve and grow that purpose so it may continue to make a difference in each person's life you touch. Embrace the adversity, because with Greatness comes much responsibility, but also Rewards.

—Ase'

Contents

Introduction

I began thinking of this book while I was sitting in deep meditation and reflecting on my self-progress. I thought that I would like to share my gifts of transformation with the world. It's funny when regarding our life experiences that we sometimes don't think of them as transformations, but they are. Every good, bad, or even traumatic experience that you've ever had has shaped and molded you into the person you are today. What would happen if we pushed those limits to not only grow from those experiences but also to elevate our mental capacity and spiritual selves so that we might serve a bigger purpose, other than just getting through circumstances?

I remember waking up one morning. I can't remember the exact date, but I remember the time. It was 11:11 a.m., which ironically is a huge divine number that stands for change, paying attention to your thoughts, new ideas, staying positive, and listening to your intuition. So at 11:11 a.m., I was lying in bed with my frantic thoughts and fears. I had just started dating a new guy, and I kept thinking of how unfulfilled I felt about our progress and connection.

Don't get me wrong; I really liked this man and wanted to put in the effort to connect with him emotionally. But I felt that I may have been forcing things instead of letting them unfold organically. You see, I have major control issues. Unfortunately, I used to be fixated on people and things that I couldn't control. The good thing is that I was aware of this flaw. We will get into becoming more self-aware later on in this book. Nevertheless, I kept thinking about what I was actually requiring from this guy, and something dawned on me: The universe might just be telling me to look deeper within myself. Or maybe the universe was yelling at me to look deeper within myself to find the comfort and satisfaction that I was seeking from this man.

I began to write down all of my desires and what I really wanted and was seeking from this man. I decided to dissect them and look further into myself to determine what I was actually asking for from another human being. As my thoughts began to come rapidly, I wrote down *six* expectations, which were: healthy communication, being made a priority, affection, intimacy, safety, and honesty. I know you may be asking yourself, *How in the hell can I give myself these things?* The answer is that you set your intentions to what you desire and follow through with them. Although I still wanted comfort from that individual, the universe told me that what I really wanted something deeper, which I could obtain. So I decided to write down healthy solutions that I could pour into myself and my energy. These solutions could give me the same satisfaction that I'd have if I were with this guy.

One desire was for healthy communication. My healthy solution was to set a daily alarm at 4:44 p.m. (which is another divine number), and meditate on my thoughts and feelings. I knew that meditation would allow me to have candid conversations with my mental state, my higher self, and God (or the universe) about where I wanted to be and what I wanted to manifest. I became powerful enough to solve my insecurities, often just through meditation.

Next, I wanted to be made a priority of by the person I admired. The problem was that I needed someone else's validation to make me feel important. So my healthy solution to this consisted of something simple: do something nice for myself (go to lunch, buy a pair of shoes, get my nails done, and do other activities like that).

Another big desire that I needed to fulfill was affection. I longed for it and really enjoyed being loved on by that certain individual. My solution was to set another daily alarm at 2:22 p.m. (Yep, you guessed it; it's another divine number) so that I could give myself a positive word of affirmation. This meant that every day I would look at myself in the mirror and say something nice about myself: complimenting the way I looked that day, setting boundaries between me and the people in my life, or just giving myself a pat on the back for doing a good job. It would make me feel good.

Some may think that this is a little egotistical or even

a narcissistic approach to gaslight your ego. But the truth is that people don't give themselves enough praise. You navigate through this world by working for another person's dream or nurturing someone else's ego, but you neglect your own. Unfortunately before you know it, you have certain insecurities about yourself or feel neglected in general and don't know the reason for it. So I always suggest taking a moment to pour love into yourself before you pour it into anyone else. This includes your husband, your children, friends, etc. If you're not your own best self, how can you be at your best for someone else?

Next up on the list of my desires was intimacy. My healthy solution to this was masturbation. That's right! I would give myself some good ole alone time to explore my body, release unwanted energy, and feel good. Although we shall dive more into masturbation and the way that it's an ultimate contributor to self-love in upcoming chapters, just know that masturbation is healthy, normal, and warranted for your mental state.

Second to last on my desire list was safety. As a single woman, I kept asking myself if I could physically protect myself if someone tried to harm me. As women, we really appreciate the protection and security of men. When a confident and strong man is around, you feel safe and almost invincible—as if nothing can harm you. Since I couldn't feel this way unless I had a man present, I knew that I needed to do some work on myself. I needed to give myself my own safety and security. So I decided to invest in some self-defense classes and beef up some of my defense and protective systems, such as mace, a Taser, and a pocket knife to carry around with me. Are you thinking this was too extreme? I don't think so. A woman's safety is nothing to play with, and during the time of COVID-19 and killer hornets, I figured a little self-defense class couldn't hurt.

Lastly my final desire was to have complete honesty. I required honesty from anyone who was in my life, but I wasn't always honest to myself about the situations I put myself in. So my healthy solution was to hold myself accountable for my actions and give myself harsh realities of truth, which I might have run away from in the past. I would need to be self-aware of actions that took me completely out of character and my higher self. I needed to call myself out on it!

It's a different story when you hold yourself accountable instead of someone else's opinions dictating who you are. But this also gives you a liberated feeling because you'll always do it with love for yourself. You can be stern with yourself but not harsh—don't demean your pride. Remember, this is about self-love and healing. In addition, you feel good about it because you've pushed yourself to do and be better. You never allow someone else to tell you who you are because you're already aware of your power and what you possess. So let's do some healing.

Chapter 1

Who Are You?

Identifying who you are and what you want out of life is essential when navigating the universe. Some may find the go-with-the-flow approach relatively satisfying, but I do not. Where are you flowing with no plan or destination in mind? This leads me to say that you must clearly state your affirmations and focus on them if you want them to manifest in the ways that you expect them to.

While growing up, people always associated me with what I had accomplished instead of who I really was. Now, I'm a successful TV producer who's made a name for herself and climbed the ladder of adversity in every way, but that's not who I am. I started working on redefining myself outside of my career a few years ago. I learned that a career was not a safe haven for my individuality. Although, sometimes others wanted to define me by my accolades, I had to set the boundaries within myself.

I have accomplished a lot of things in my short time as

an adult, but *I am not* only my accomplishments. *I am* a spiritual being who is protected by God, the universe and my ancestors. I love to spread love and light to those in need. I am super aware of my superpowers and the way that true affirmations can manifest in my life.

Let's define what affirmations are. Affirmations are pure intentions and goals that you affirm will happen or be completed. For instance, if you have a small business, you create an affirmation that it will make $3,000 in one month and put in the work. If you also have faith that you will accomplish this goal and that you've successfully fulfilled this promise to yourself, you have manifested what your heart and mind have desired. Affirmations are also positive life-giving words that you speak to yourself, friends, or other people that you care about.

Because we are focused on self-love, I want to share one of my own positive affirmations that I speak to myself: "I am a beautifully flawed woman who has healed from previous pain and trauma and who is on a path to enlightenment."

When you set your affirmations in the universe and truly put your faith in yourself, God, the universe, and anything else you believe in, you become one of the most powerful forces on the planet. I say that because you will then have an unwavering love and dedication, which you've found within yourself. When you become self-aware of your power, you begin to identify and understand who you are and what you want to accomplish in this lifetime. The power within yourself is limitless, but it comes over time. It's nurtured by self-love affirmations and positive, healthy mental spaces.

It can take years to tap into your higher energy's frequencies. Every individual has a frequency. It's like a radio. We, as humans, feed off each other's energies and frequencies. We can feel when people are on high frequencies because they exude confidence and they're genuinely happy with themselves. It doesn't mean that they don't have challenges, but they've learned ways to stay positive while going through the obstacles. People who are on high frequencies also have clear understandings of who they are and what they want out of life. You generally feel good when you're around them.

Individuals who display low frequencies or vibrations are typically not themselves. Their energy is heavy and sometimes negative. You can feel a thick tension when you stand next to a person with low vibrations. Now keep in mind that a person can alternate between low and high frequencies at certain times of the day or during weeks, months, years and so on. But it's all about balance. We will dive more deeply into low and high frequencies later on in this book. These frequencies enable you to learn who you are and how you want to show up in this universe.

I'll tell you a story or few about my journey in learning about myself—the heartbreak, depression, highs, and lows. I needed to have some real conversations with myself and hold myself accountable for a lot of the unhealed trauma and pain that I seemed to have never dealt with. Do you remember how in the beginning I mentioned pouring love into the desires I wanted met by a man, even though I knew that I was capable of also providing myself with these things? I learned that giving your pain and heartache a voice can be a powerful healing outlet. That's right. Identify your past hurt, which you've most likely tucked away in your subconscious and buried with other convoluted thoughts, and give it a voice!

On the journey of finding out and understanding who I was and where I wanted to be, all the painful events of my heart being broken, being taken advantage of and experiencing extreme losses that I didn't deal with, I gave a voice to, and scream about during a meditation session I was having. I set in motion a pure, heavy, and negative energy release for myself. I lit some candles, reached into my Tibetan music collection, sat in a dimly lit space in my meditation room, and screamed my pain into the universe.

I hurt because I had lost of a child, been in domestic and emotionally abusive relationships with a man, woman, friend, foe, and family member, who had taken me for granted and betrayed my trust. I hurt because I had been bullied and was never quite accepted. All of my devastations came flooding out my mouth like hot lava violently erupting from a volcano. It was liberating, it was sad, but it was me!

I did this release for two hours in my meditation room. I felt lethargic afterward, but I was also relieved to have unleashed the mental and emotional hell that I had created for myself. I allowed myself to simply feel the things that I had buried. It made me feel stronger and gave me the power to take accountability over my life and my expectations for life.

Happiness and maintaining an upward frequency elevation are always at the forefront of my mind. But it takes an enormous amount of energy to continue to operate in your higher self (best version of yourself).

There's power in pain and the facing of that pain. The Dalai Lama, a great leader in the spiritual realm, said, "Happiness is not something ready made. It comes from your own actions." You have to put in the work so that you can process your trauma and unhealed wounds. Then you will gain much clarity on your identity.

I want you to do an exercise on your own. Practice writing your own positive affirmations in the blank spaces below. Feed love and life into yourself, your business, or anything that you need to reassure yourself about, such as an extra push to keep you on the positive path to your own enlightenment and spiritual freedom. Here is an example: "Today, I invite peace, unconditional love, money, and positive energy into my life."

Create Your Own Affirmations Exercise

1. _____

2. _____

3. _____

4. _____

5. _____

6. _____

7. _____

8. _____

9. _____

10. _____

Chapter 2

Pouring Love into Your Affirmations and Unlocking Your Spiritual Power

Now that you've established what your affirmations are, how are you going to nurture them and make sure that they manifest? Let's discuss the energy that you possess when you achieve your manifestations. All affirmations require love, focus, and positive energy. You may not understand what I mean when I tell you to pour love into your affirmations, so allow me to clarify. Affirmations are the thoughts, desires, and goals that you seek and want to manifest or come to reality. Manifesting your affirmations takes a great deal of energy. You must surround yourself with positive energy to stay the course. I'm not saying that negative energy can't also propel your manifestations, but you want your energy to be in the right place. Negative energy will do nothing but drain your focus and create low vibrations.

In the past when I've set my affirmations, I have

purposefully aligned myself with the right resources and energy that will allow me to always think of the bigger picture. Pouring love into your affirmations means giving them a voice, speaking them out loud, and owning the reassurance that you're going to accomplish and manifest these desires. You begin to write them down, pray over them, and ultimately, do the work. For instance, if you're a single man or woman seeking marriage and long-term companionship, you become more mindful of where your energy spreads. This means that you date with a purpose. You set your intentions on seeking and connecting to a soul mate, and you're not afraid to shed connections or potential mates who no longer serve you or your affirmation to obtain this.

It means being fearless enough to take the leap of faith, weed out the roads that aren't right for you, and stay steadfast in your affirmations by doing the work. I know this seems like an easy task because I'm telling you to write down your dreams, focus on them, and then achieve them. However, even I know all too well that it's not that easy to manifest your affirmations to fruition. In fact, it's hard as hell. It takes discipline and sacrifice, and it can cause emotional trauma that you never saw coming your way. By you setting your intentions to pour into your affirmations so that they will come true and you will have no choice but to move forward.

Pouring love into affirmations is loving yourself unconditionally because you want your affirmations to win and even exceed your heart's desires. I'll tell you a secret about myself and a snippet of my journey in my television career. Back in 2014, I set my intentions to transition from working as a radio producer for one of the top urban stations in Chicago to a production assistant in the television industry. Although I graduated with a bachelor's degree in radio and television, I still had no idea what it took to break into the television industry.

Now those who know me know that I'm determined, and some may even call me fearless. I saw an opportunity to sit in the audience of a prominent, well-known television show that was filming in Chicago. I told myself before I reserved tickets for this show that I was going to get a meeting and connect with someone who could assist me in my affirmation. I reserved the tickets and got a phone call from the audience coordinator a few days later.

The audience coordinator and I connected while on the phone. He had great energy. My inner self said, *What the hell. Just go for it*, so as he gave me the information about attending this show's event, I asked him if he could connect me with someone that could help me transition from radio to the television world. I heard a slight pause and a deep breath on the phone. I sat there holding the phone to my ear and wondering if I had just messed up the vibe so that he would reject my request and blow me off. All of these negative thoughts flooded my head.

Then I heard him say, "Sure. I'd love to connect you with our production coordinator after the show. Bring a few copies of your resume and cover letter, and I'll see what I can do." I was elated. I jumped up and down as my heart beat out of my chest. I was grateful. I had the confidence in myself to know that I would do what I needed to do to make sure that I worked on that show and made the right impression on that production coordinator. Now don't get me wrong. There were no guarantees that I would even see this person, but I didn't allow my mind to focus on negative what-if's. Instead, I knew that I had to do my part and come prepared for anything, even if I was only an audience member. I saw myself being more and seized an opportunity.

Now let's fast-forward. The audience coordinator did keep his word and introduced me to the production coordinator, to whom I was able to give my resume and from whom I got his contact information. The audience coordinator even gave me front-row seats and an exclusive VIP option to take pictures on the set. It was all surreal, and I was so grateful. But the story didn't end there.

Although the production coordinator gave me his information, he never answered my calls. I know. What a bummer that is, right? However, I was determined to make contact because I knew what type of worker I was. I knew that the spirit and energy I possessed to make things happen for myself wouldn't be denied, and even if it was, I knew that I would keep going anyway. I called the production coordinator for one straight year, every day, and sometimes twice a day. I left voice mails with a brief description of who I was to ensure that he'd remember me. And on the day my spirit was beginning to get weary, I called him again, and *he answered.* That's right. After 365 days, minus weekends and holidays, he finally answered my phone call and told me to come in on the following week because he was going to start me off as a backstage PA for the show.

I was so excited that I couldn't breathe. I finally got the opportunity that I had been affirming as a manifestation. My spirit and will hadn't even allowed me to think that I couldn't do this. An even bigger icing on the cake was that the production coordinator's boss saw my work ethic and referred me for a full-time production assistant position. I spent three and a half years with that show and that team. I received two promotions and won a Daytime Emmy Award. I still owe a lot of my accomplishments today to that team and show.

I poured a huge amount of love, preparation, and persistence into that affirmation, but it was worth it. Of course, I'm not saying that you have to take any of the routes that helped me. But I told my story so that you might understand that manifestations and affirmations can be successful and liberating with the right energy. I didn't have to pray about my affirmations every day or even every week. I wrote my affirmations down, prayed about them, released them into the universe, and said that they would come to fruition. You don't have to pray or meditate on your affirmations every day for them to hold the power to manifest. You just need to believe them and trust the process, God, and the universe that they will be. I hate to sound cliché, but what's for you will be for you, and there's nothing anyone can do about it because it's your own divine calling.

Now let's talk about restoring your energy so that you can keep pouring love into your affirmations and not get weary or discouraged when the timing is not happening at your needed pace. Just like any other normal person, your mind, spirit, and body can get weary and begin to drift into a place of hopelessness. Don't let it! Here's how you stay vigilant and vibrant in your affirmations. I call this my Affirmation-Boost Method. It's when you make a point of rejuvenating your spirit to ensure the success of your manifestation.

Affirmation-Boost Method

1. Remember to pour love into yourself through self-care days and by surrounding yourself with positive energy and loved ones who know you will accomplish your goals. You have to learn how to energize your spirit. You do that by surrounding yourself with things that make you feel good and wanted and ensure your purpose in life. Your spirit may feel weary, but those around you can see things that you may have neglected.

2. Utilize your network or even get a different network and find success stories that are similar to yours. By doing this, you create a sense of realism. You'll be able to understand that things really do come in time. This will also allow you to understand the mentality of one who prepares and has patience. In fact, that's actually the third step.

3. Patience is the big key to staying steadfast. Sometimes I even had to pray for patience so that I would remain focused and not lose my drive. I hate to use another cliché, but, "Great things come to those who wait." This statement is true to a certain extent because once you've written your affirmations and released them to the universe, your efforts to align yourself come and ensure your readiness for your affirmations to manifest. The time that they will manifest is out of your control; however, your faith will reassure you that it will indeed manifest. Do you know why? It's because you've put in the work and believed that your efforts will be noticed.

My all-time favorite movie is *The Matrix*. I absolutely love it, not only for it being an impressive and thrilling sci-fi film but also because of its hidden gems, which unfold throughout the movie. If you've never watched *The Matrix*, it's OK. My brief interpretation will allow you some insight. The movie takes us on an adventure with a young protégé named Neo, a man who has grown weary of the monotonous life he's been living. Then he gets an invitation from a well-known cyber activist called Morpheus to rescue him from his mundane lifestyle by freeing his mind of the alternate reality he knows as The Matrix. Morpheus believes with his whole heart and mind that Neo is *the one*, and he has invested his entire life into rescuing Neo. Morpheus believes that Neo will be the messiah that their chained world has needed. Morpheus knows that he only needs to pour positive reinforcements into Neo to get him to believe in himself and that Neo will be able to do extraordinary things once his mind is set free and he believes what he is capable of. Essentially, Neo finds himself being challenged to accept that the only world he's ever known has been a figment of a system's imagination, which has used it to control the minds of its citizens and keep them in captivity and governed by rules. Therefore, it limits their successes and possibilities of what they can actually accomplish.

Neo finds himself second-guessing his decisions but knows that Morpheus has seen something in him that Neo hasn't seen. He doesn't want to let Morpheus down.

I love the Matrix's whole concept: to live your life without boundaries, rules, or regulations, which have been reinforced by the normality of society as we know it. In addition, the movie's narrative perpetuates a life of freeing your mind and becoming self-aware that you can manifest anything that you put your mind to.

At the end of the movie, a skeptical Neo becomes a

believer. He is in fact the messiah. He has gained the confidence to defeat all systematic barriers and enemies who are preventing him from walking in his true purpose. Neo then begins to do extraordinary things like stopping bullets with his hand, having extraordinary speed, and possessing a whole slew of additional gifts he never thought that he was capable of having.

I used this analogy to reinforce what it means to pour into your affirmations and be so focused on them to manifest that the universe has no choice but to bestow blessings on you. You so blindly believe that your affirmations will come to fruition that nothing can get in the way. Honestly, that's what unlocking your spiritual power is about—the ability to will something to manifest blindly but also with a purpose.

At the end of this book, I want you to keep challenging yourself to pour into your affirmations and lay your own foundations so that your manifestations can be in abundance. The foundations you lay for yourself contribute to the amount of self-love and preservation you deserve.

Chapter 3

Self-Love Affirmations and Meditation

Self-Love is one of the best gifts that you can give yourself. It will ensure the confidence and liberation that you will need to believe in the goals that you want to manifest. Oftentimes, I've given my friends self-love advice and created self-love affirmations for myself. Let's be real. *We* can be our own worst critics and come down really hard on ourselves. This tears down our self-esteem, morals and confidence. Becoming self-aware of the trauma that we have inflicted on ourselves can create a toxic mentality and unhealthy space for yourself and your thoughts. We must learn to reprogram those thoughts and turn them into positivity and unconditional love for the people whom we are as individuals and are aspiring to be during a growth season.

Be honest with yourself. When was the last time you poured pure love into yourself, gave yourself a self-care day, or appreciated your own presence without anyone else around. Self-care is pivotal in maintaining and rejuvenating your positive energy so that all your heart's desires will get spiritually fed and nourished.

There's a book by Ward Farnsworth entitled *Farnsworth's Classical English Rhetoric.* Farnsworth says that people have "an appetite for well-expressed wisdom, motivational or otherwise." My interpretation of this quote is that people naturally crave positivity and motivation. Because of the world that we live in and those whom we surround ourselves with, we may not always get the positive motivation or support that we need on our individual journeys. Therefore, self-love affirmations are a necessity. People should allow themselves the opportunity to just love on themselves.

Below, there are some personal yet effective mantras and affirmations that I've not only created for myself but also for some of my friends so that they can pour love into themselves. They ensure that the universe will gravitate and attract the type of energy that you want surrounding you. By all means, you can create your own daily mantras, which will be uniquely designed to you, but if you need a quick jolt of love, you can find it in these.

Daily Self-Love Affirmation to Heal Trauma

- I am good enough.
- I am not the same broken person that I was in my last relationship or experience.
- I can handle any situation that the universe throws at me because I am strong enough!
- I am and will be an awesome parent.
- I deserve unconditional love
- I love myself unconditionally and even when others don't.
- I will always protect myself and my children.
- I will set boundaries in my relationships with lovers and friends.
- I will attract nothing but positive energy and people with pure intentions into my life.
- I AM A SURVIVOR!!

Daily Self-Love Affirmation for Strength

- I am strength.
- I will no longer have a toxic mentality that tears down who I am.
- I embrace the person that I am today.
- I love hard, but I love me harder.
- I will not sacrifice myself or my security to make others happy.
- I can handle anything that the universe throws at me now.
- I am aware of my power and all that I possess.
- I am a spiritual being who's protected by God, the universe, and my ancestors.
- I am so proud of me and the positive progression that I've made as this person.
- I can give myself everything that a man/woman can, and my happiness will not be based on someone else.

Daily Self-Love Affirmation for New Journeys

- I will not allow anyone to steal my joy during this new season of my life.
- I am surrounded by unconditional love and support from people who only want the best for me.
- God will continue to bless me and my future union with peace and abundant love.
- I will no longer stress over the little things because they have no control over my destiny.
- I am marrying my best friend and life partner.
- I will have faith that everything will work out.
- This is my season, and not everyone will be allowed on my journey.
- I am worthy of unconditional support and understanding.
- I can handle anything that the universe throws at me because I am protected and surrounded by God and my ancestors.

Daily Self-Love Affirmation for Money

- I attract an abundant amount of blessings into my life.
- I am ready for an overflow of money, opportunities, and financial freedom
- I will be debt free.
- I will continue on my path to create generational wealth and financial security.
- I appreciate all abundance that is given to me by God, my ancestors, and the universe.
- I love money, and money loves me too.

Daily Self-Love Affirmation for Protection

- I affirm that nothing but positive energy will surround me and my life.
- I am protected by God, my ancestors, and my spiritual guides.
- I affirm that nothing negative will penetrate my soul or spirit because I am surrounded by love and guardianship.
- My thoughts, body, and energy are protected from any negativity.
- I am protected by positive energy and unconditional love.
- I affirm that I am in a safe spiritual space and surrounded by pure protection and security.

Blessings to you! I hope that these affirmations will bring love and light to all who read and affirm them to the universe so that these affirmations will manifest at the time that is right for you. Namaste.

Self-Care Regimens

Not only do affirmations play a huge and significant part in healing and gaining self-love but they are also essential to a person's psyche and well-being. Self-care regimens are designed to restore your energy. During life's chaotic times and when you're feeling the pressures of the world on your shoulders, they give you moments to breathe. I've composed a list of daily, weekly, and monthly self-care regimens that you can use, or you can make your own. Either way, it is essential for you to have a regimen to restore yourself. I have even gone on a seven-day spiritual fast to reinforce my spiritual powers and cleanse my spirit of unwarranted energies.

Self-Care Ideas

Monthly full body massages
Biweekly nail (fingernails and/or toenails) appointment
Daily/weekly meditation and prayer session
Random shopping trips for gifts
Masturbation
Mirror work - Speaking positive affirmations to yourself in the mirror

Space from others to reflect and re-center yourself

My Seven-Day Spiritual Fast

This is my cleansing process that allows me to give up something of importance or of pleasure to me i.e., my favorite food, social media, spending less money on luxuries or whatever you feel will be a sacrifice for you. This process is like what someone may do for lent, but you can determine the duration of the fast. Afterwards I would set my intentions on what I wanted to accomplish, which is to power my manifestations and allow me to be closer to God. This is how I did that in addition to fasting. As a reminder this is all subjective and you can do what you feel will work for you.

Day 1

Clear your mind and state your intentions to have a successful business.

Day 2

Focus on your self-worth and development and ask for signs and answers for clarity regarding your love life while wearing your yoni egg.

Day 3

Re-center your focus and energy on yourself and your purpose.

Day 4

Shed your insecurities.

Day 5

Love yourself, practice giving yourself compliments throughout the day, and do not be harsh with yourself.

Day 6

Cleanse yourself: Eat clean, meditate, and wear your yoni egg.

Day 7

Show gratefulness to your ancestors and God. Conduct a thankful ceremony, take a smudge bowl, light pure white candles around your intimate space or alter, grab a clear glass of fresh clean water, burn you some ancestry money or joss paper and place into the smudge bowl. The joss paper is a representation of an offering to your ancestors. The paper can represent all the things you are grateful for i.e., good health, financial stability, unconditional love, etc... The purpose of this is to show that you are grateful and paying homage to the ancestral energy that's surrounding you.

Some may be asking what a yoni egg is. The term *yoni* is a nice, sophisticated way of describing your vagina or vulva. The yoni is especially used as a symbol of divine procreative energy, which is conventionally designed as a circular stone or crystal that you insert into your vagina. It has been said that yoni eggs provide great healing powers and ground and create a healthy cleaning magnetism for your uterus.

My spiritual fast helped me get closer to God and my ancestors and spiritually fed me the things that I needed to know about myself and to still heal from. During this season of fasting, I gained the clarity that I needed regarding unresolved situations in my life. I received additional finances and blessings and became more mentally sound. Just to elaborate, on Day 3 of my spiritual fast, I received a random check for $2,000. I distinctly remember that during my meditation I asked for abundant blessings and continued financial security. Later that day, I received a wire transfer of $2,000 from an organization that I am a part of. The wire said that I had been randomly selected to be funded this amount of money.

I know that other people may have testimonies of God working in mysterious ways, but by far, this was only one of the many blessings that were bestowed on me after I had connected more spiritually. So I say all of that to show that manifesting is real, not just because of the unforeseen blessings but because I was tapping into my God power, which allowed me to live and receive the treasures of life that I wanted.

Candle Magic and Rootwork

Since the dawn of time of in ancient Africa, rootwork (better known as hoodoo) has been a pivotal reinforcement of manifestations. Now before anyone gets uptight or on edge, this is not a book of sorcery or demonic energy; however, it is ideal for one to know the history of hoodoo and harnessing spiritual magic. The short answer is that it came from our ancestors. In past years, slaves adapted to spiritual rituals and traditions because they had come into Native American and European cultures. There's a very interesting book by Angelie Belard called *Hoodoo for Beginners*, which is a great read for those who need to do more research and get more in tune with old folk magic from our ancestors.

I mention these methods to explain how in-depth spiritual powers go if you're willing to tap into them. Candle magic is a form of rootwork; however, it is a reinforcement of the manifestations that you seek to affirm in the universe. There are several different candles with vibrant colors and essential meanings that you can use to be more direct in what you're manifesting.

For instance, a white candle promotes serenity,

tranquility, and peace and enhances personal strength and insight. It is also used as cleansing mechanism which clears out unwarranted energies and replaces them with purities. It is also great for paying homage to your ancestors.

A black candle protects your psyche and mental space. They are also used to prohibit any wrongdoing or toxic mentality to your psyche.

A green candle helps bring your ideas to life and amplifies prosperity, especially when it comes to money. Here is just an FYI: When I manifested my $2,000, I was using a green candle to amplify this energy as I spoke abundance into my life.

A blue candle connects to your chakras; particularly your throat and heart chakras. It also helps with any emotional wounds that need healing.

A yellow candle enhances your networking and social skills and brings in new career opportunities. Typically utilizing the yellow and green candles will amplify blessings in a meditation session.

A red candle encourages love, sex, and extreme passion. I suggest that when you are saying your daily affirmations, you should light a red or yellow candle to amplify your signal to the universe. In return, it gives you the confidence you'll need when you're affirming.

A pink candle is also utilized for romance and new friendships. A pink candle welcomes new love and overwhelming bliss into your life.

A purple candle boosts your spiritual enlightenment and creativity. Purple is also the color of your crown chakra, which steers stillness, grounding, and divine awareness into your body and spirit.

An orange candle encourages your ambition and helps you broaden your horizons. It also speaks to your sacral chakra, which helps with emotional balance and synchronicity.

Lastly, a brown candle helps with all things relating to your internal source. Some examples of this are your health, energy, pets, endurance, and courage.

I strongly suggest exploring candle magic. Find out the great wonders that await you during your next prayer or meditation session.

The REM-Sleep Realm

I am a huge self-care advocate who believes that you should cater to your spirit and yourself in every aspect of life—even while you sleep. I believe that while you sleep, you can pour into yourself and your affirmations through your subconscious.

You've likely heard that while you sleep, your mind slips into the deepest parts of your subconscious, which allows you to have dreams and experience circumstances outside of this reality. My interpretation of your dream (REM) state is defined as the most active part of your sleep state. Your eyes move rapidly, unbeknownst to you. REM typically stimulates the areas of the brain that help you with learning. REM is associated with the increased production of proteins in the body. In addition, it's where your dreams can begin to manifest. REM taps into a higher sense of the subconscious, which we cannot control or understand.

However, I believe that certain spiritual powers can be achieved and harnessed through your REM state of sleep just like meditation can. For instance, meditating is a technical way of being able to calm your mind and energy. This helps you focus on relaxing your body in the way that you need to so that you can feel at peace. Sleep is so important to the body because it helps to restore and rejuvenate it physically as well as mentally.

I can testify that once I became diligent and intentional in my meditations, I opened a whole new door to my subconscious self (my higher self) and began to learn how to affirm my goal even while I was in my deepest sleep. I asked God and my spirit guides to provide me with the clarity and willingness to affirm my manifestations and to stay steadfast in my efforts.

My most creative ideas come to me during the state of sleep. I came up with the concept for my clothing boutique and the audience that I wanted to cater to. I came up with chapter titles for this book during that state of sleep. I even manifested a specific amount of money, which was deposited into my account two days after I spoke it to the universe. Now, don't get me wrong. I am not saying that this will always happen or that it's something you can turn on or off like a light switch. However, my point is that when you are putting in the work within yourself as well as laying down the foundation for your goals, great things can manifest through that. Meditation is an essential key to tapping into that strength.

There are four different stages to meditation. These stages allow you to peel back layers of yourself and your subconscious, be more confident in yourself, and really have faith that you can manifest anything that you put your mind to.

The first stage is the physical body. This is the preliminary stage, where you start meditating and are only in tune with or feel your physical body. You feel yourself sitting in a stance or lying down, the breath enter and exit your body, and even the warmth or chills that spread over your body as you lie there.

The second stage of meditation is when you tap into your emotional state. This is where you dive a little deeper and encounter your emotional self. You are checking your emotional temperature to see if you are feeling anxious, overwhelmed, happy, fearful, or emotionally exhausted, which comes from feeling all the emotions at one time. In this stage of mediation, you begin to educate yourself on how you're feeling and give those feelings a voice so that they can be cleansed or regulated.

During the third stage of meditation, you try to find higher self-guidance. This is the stage where you're essentially tapped into your subconscious. In your mind, you are in tune with your senses and know how to silence it. You experience ways to isolate those heavy emotions that you sorted through in stage two. Now your subconscious is wide awake, and it has emerged.

This stage is essentially a version of the REM sleep state. Your physical body may be in a relaxed state, but your mind is active, and you're able to speak life into your goals and affirmations. In this sleep realm, you begin to visualize yourself in a higher position or state of success, which you have been working to achieve. In my honest opinion, this is one of the most important stages of meditation to be in because you are harnessing your power to tell the universe what you want to accomplish subconsciously. In itself, that is powerful!

The final stage is the union of becoming light. This is the stage where your seven chakras become aligned, purified, and strengthened with the universe. Your spiritual self has literally united with God and your ancestors. This may be the stage where you can physically speak to and see your ancestors or spiritual guides. You've been able to elevate your spiritual self to a realm of spiritual connections, which you have accessed to start actually seeing your affirmations come to light. It's the superpower of clairvoyance and predicting when you'll see your success or affirmation come to fruition.

Create Your Own Affirmations Exercise

1. _____

2. _____

3. _____

4. _____

5. _____

6. _____

7. _____

8. _____

9. _____

10. _____

Chapter 4

Channeling Your
Masculine and Feminine Energies

The concept of duality is in each and every person. However, the amount of masculine and feminine energy that one person can have will be different for each individual.

Let's define the two energies and learn their purposes. *The Merriam-Webster Dictionary's* definition of masculinity states that it is a set of attributes, behaviors, and roles associated with boys and men. However, research has shown that masculinity can be socially constructed by certain behaviors and traits that can be embodied in both the male and female sexes. These traits consist of independence, courage, strength, leadership and assertiveness, to name a few.

Femininity has been defined as a set of attributes, behaviors, and roles that are generally associated with girls or women. In addition, female traits have been noted as gentleness, empathy, sensitivity, and humility. Research has also shown that these traits can also be present in masculine species such as boys or men.

What I want you to understand is that masculinity and femininity can coexist in both sexes and typically vary in its standards across other cultures. In individual interpretations and even throughout history, they both have evolved to a higher understanding, which exceeds a person's sex or gender and becomes interchangeable over time.

Let's discuss the importance of the two. Masculine and feminine energies are widely important to the makeup of any man or woman. In order to connect with your higher self or have appreciation for every part of you, you need to be self-aware of the traits that you embody and exude. As a man, you may exude more feminine traits than masculine ones. If you are a woman, you may exude more masculine traits than feminine ones.

I have become self-aware that I embody a ton of masculinity and exude those same attributes that I mentioned earlier: independence, courage, strength, leadership, and assertiveness. Growing up in a two-parent household, I often witnessed certain gender roles take place between my mom and dad. I experienced my dad, as a working-class citizen, being the provider, going to work every day, and showcasing courage, sensitivity, and strength to ensure that his family enjoyed the finer things in life. I saw my mom, who was also be a provider, go to work every day, cook dinner, clean the house, pay bills, and show independence and assertiveness. I noticed shared duties of the household being taken care of by both my mom and dad.

Some people may have the outdated ideology of the 1950s or 1960s, saying that women should take care of the household while men bring home the bacon. But the truth is that I witnessed both masculine and feminine traits from both of my parents, which then allowed me to understand that the two energies were interchangeable in men and women. I saw my dad cry and show extreme emotion. I'll admit that it was rare, but it was present. I saw my mom become extremely aggressive when it came to getting things done in a professional setting. When I became older I wanted to emulate those same traits but also define them in a more organic way and design them according to who I was.

The biggest misconception is forcing men to only exhibit masculine traits and women to only exhibit feminine traits. In reality, both traits and energies are warranted for people to be whole and to understand who they are. Ladies, can you imagine dating a man who only showcases assertiveness but has no gentleness or is courageous and daring but isn't cautious or sensitive to your feelings? Or men, can you imagine dating a woman who is only sensitive but incapable of being self-sufficient?

Feminine and masculine energies require balance. Balancing those energies is ideally up to the individual; however, too much feminine or masculine energy isn't necessarily a good thing. Equilibrium must be achieved in order to wholeheartedly understand who you are as a man or a woman.

There's a crystal called the Shiva lingam, which possesses magical powers that harness and balance your masculine and feminine energies. The stone hails from the Narmada River in Western India, one of India's most holy sites. It originates from the Indian Hindu culture. The representation of this stone emulates masculine energies through its solid oval shape and feminine energies through its many unique patterns presented on the stone. Through this formation, the stone is able to link to the forces of creation, just as humans can physically birth new life through the connection of the male and female bodies. The Shiva lingam aids in understanding polarized energies, such as male-female, light-dark, and spiritual-physical entities. It is ideally one of my favorite crystals due to the way that it exuberantly expresses duality and merges the two energies.

For years, Hindus, Buddhists, Tibetans, and others have understood how vital and essential balancing your feminine and masculine energies is; however, in Western culture, it's not talked about or explored as much. I want to change that and give you a better understanding of things that may seem taboo and will surely not be included in any history books, such as discussing the integration of masculine and feminine energies

In some cases we may know the integration to be called synergy, which is the interaction or cooperation of two or more entities to produce a combined effect and create a greater contribution together than they would independently. It results in creating something beautiful and pure for the greater cause of an individual.

Synergy is very precious in its own right, due to the impact it has on relationships and friendships alone. When any man or woman has the capacity to integrate his or her energies, I call it growth.

Chapter 5

The Art of
Manifesting while Masturbating

Now let's get on to the fun part—a chapter discussing the release of your sexual energies in a liberating way. This gets me so excited (literally)! For years in Indian cultures, sexuality has been a depiction of exuberant sexual beings exploring eroticism and sexuality in many ways.

For instance, the Kama Sutra is an ancient Indian Sanskrit text on sexuality, eroticism, and emotional fulfillment in life. For centuries, the Kama Sutra has prohibited people's inhibitions regarding how high they can explore their sexual fantasies and peaks. In this book, I want to go a step further and promote the healthy habit of masturbating and having the honor to understand your body and needs. I'm talking about being so in tune with your own sexual prowess that having a spouse or mate will only be a contribution to your life—not a necessity.

According to ancient history, the Sumerians (ancient Egypt), the Greeks, and the Romans all explored masturbation. During these ancient time frames, masturbation was used to enhance sexual experiences and potency in both men and women. We may have heard of these things before—all the wild and crazy sex parties that the Greeks used to have, which always made me envy their wild liberation. Masturbation is an essential part of history, and it was one of the more iconic ways for ancient beings to elevate their spiritual powers. Masturbation is an extremely healthy outlet to release unwanted energy and enhance self-love for your own spirit, body, and mind.

In the picture below, you will find an ancient-Greek Satyr, which was a male nature spirit that emulated the physical appearance of a horse with an exaggerated erection. He's depicted as masturbating. The picture was captured in 560–550 BC, according to Wikipedia's records.

I wanted to showcase images like these to make people aware that it is no longer taboo to explore their bodies. I utilize masturbation as one of my superpowers. Let me explain. Being aware of yourself and your spirit so that you can tap into your superpowers is a huge gift from the universe and your ancestors. In order to have the capacity to elevate yourself spiritually as a human being, you must explore and connect deeply with who you are internally. Masturbation can offer you that liberation and internal power.

I used to lie in bed at night with my head in the clouds. I was full of good and bad emotions. My anxiety used to always get the best of me, and many nights, it caused me to have insomnia. Until one night when I decided to center my thoughts and essentially masturbate to the thoughts that wouldn't allow me to sleep. As I began my session, I set my intention to release the unwanted feelings and energies that were occupying my headspace. At the point of my climax, I envisioned myself with a clear head and consciousness and released those thoughts that were contributing to my anxiety and fear. To be honest, it was the most liberating feeling that I've ever felt in my life! I felt calmer, I felt free, and most of all, I actually released those thoughts that were keeping me up at night.

I challenge you to set your intentions for anything that you do in life, including masturbation. I utilized masturbation as a tool to release unwanted energies but also to reinforce my own self-love. As I would touch myself on a consistent basis, I would explore my body in a more elevated way. I learned to love every crevice of myself from the inside to the outside. I know that some people may think I'm crazy. A woman freely talking about masturbating and touching herself on a consistent basis is unheard of, right? But despite judgement or maybe lack of understanding, challenge yourself to explore your own body and mind in a more intentional way. I am asking you to take the chaos that is brewing in your head, apply it to your body, and then release it while you're at your highest peak of an orgasm. You will reach pure serendipity.

Here is a fun fact: Oftentimes when I meditate, I enjoy listening to music that is serene and promotes me to transcend my mind. Typically the music is soft, with use of chimes, natural sounds, and horns. But I also include Kama Sutra inspired music, which includes the sounds of moans, screams of pleasure, and ecstasy. It actually aids as an aphrodisiac to center my chakras. The soft moans that can be heard from the music allow my sacral chakra to ignite. Essentially, I can tap into my sexual prowess during a meditation session as well.

Imagine that in Indian culture, they used to get themselves right to the point of climax during masturbation and then stop before ejaculation. That's right. They actually held in their climax to solidify the control of their minds and bodies. They also wanted to create a higher potency and frequency for when they did finally release it. That way, it was more satisfying but also empowering. It was a method that was used to liberate their minds and bodies on the path to enlightenment. Just imagine the amount of power that you would retain by being able to control your orgasms—until you wanted to release them. It's empowering and daring at the same time.

The Art of Manifesting while Masturbating Itself

We've already discussed rootwork and candle magic, but what if we applied those actions to our most vulnerable but also heightened mental and physical peaks. The power of a climactic ending to an internal and individual sexual experience is underrated. There is a ton of energy that surrounds a person who's orgasming. Imagine if you yelled out your goals during each climax. Harnessing the power of liberation through a climatic experience can elevate your affirmations to another level. As a matter of fact, here's how you set the mood.

1. You'll Need Meditation Music

We've already discussed how meditation music can really enhance an experience if you allow yourself to zone out to it.

2. Light Intentional Candles

Intentional candles (candle magic) can be purchased at any spiritual store, or you can simply use white candles. White candles represent the purity of the universe, and they are symbolic of connecting with the spirit realm.

3. Unclothe Yourself and Feel Your Entire Naked Body

You want to get a sense of texture regarding how your body feels. How warm is it? How aroused do your genitalia become? What are sensations surround it? Remember that this is about loving every crevice of your body and harnessing your manifestation power.

4. Set Your Intentions

Set you intentions on where you see yourself in the next two years, five years, and hell, maybe ten years. It just depends on the goals you want to achieve and how much you will them to be manifested.

5. Begin the Act of Masturbating

As you begin to feel good with every stroke or pulse, you imagine yourself in that success. You envision yourself being successful and having everything that you want to achieve. It's basically like seeing yourself in a dream state, only it's the better version of yourself.

6. Start to Voice Your Goals Out Loud

Here's what I shouted out: "I will make six figures," "I will have eternal and everlasting love," "I will have healthy black children," and, "All my businesses will be successful." And then …

7. You Climax

You feel extremely liberated and have an ancestry energy pulsating through your body that you've never felt before, but it is so warranted. Afterward, drink a glass of wine, smoke a cigarette or even something more potent to bring yourself down, and then just reflect.

Chapter 6

Triggers

Throughout life, we are given tests to see how well we endure adversity in our lives. But during and even after overcoming these tests and extremely difficult situations, we never discuss how traumatic the events were. There's something to be said about pushing through these situations and not having something triggered in us so that we have to go through them again. Traumatic experiences can contribute to building character; however if you're not careful, your triggers to those experiences can actually hinder you from elevating yourself.

My friends would say that I have had a trying dating pattern and some challenging relationships in the past. During these times, I've gone through a ton of disappointments, heartaches, and failures, when it comes to matters of the heart. Throughout these experiences, triggers have been developed. Let me explain. Everyone has triggers. Triggers are simply recalls of emotions that weren't too pretty in life. They may have caused you to spiral downward. Triggers come without warning and flashing lights, which would tell your brain to brace itself for an emotional typhoon that will hit you like a ton of bricks emotionally and leave you to pick up the pieces and put your mental space together once you've worked through that trigger. Triggers are a form of PTSD (post-traumatic stress disorder).

The biggest contributors to triggers are lost love, betrayal, sexual trauma, and heartbreak. Scientifically, love releases the chemical dopamine and the hormone norepinephrine into your system every time you experience these serendipitous moments. These chemicals contribute to your giddy mood and create a euphoric energy that circulates throughout your body. So scientifically, your logic and mental coherency are affected by your emotions and heart chakra. I mention this because you can make some dumb and irrational decisions when you're in love. But when that love doesn't pan out the way you desired and heartbreak arises, it can lead to a detrimental state for your emotions and mentality.

Unfortunately for me, heartbreak is a pain that I've experienced all too many times. I was always the good girl, the one who waited to have sex, the one who didn't want to rush things, and the one who always followed her heart. Whew! My emotions got me into a few entanglements that I should've never been in.

I met my first heartbreaker in 2009. For confidential purposes, I'll just call him Mr. D. Mr. D gave me my first dose of reality: men lie *a lot*, their insecurities get the best of them, and their demons catch up with them. And if you're not careful, a person can bring you down right along with them. During the time that we were dating, I was in college. I think that I was in my junior year when I connected with this young man. He really had an unexpected effect on me.

I should have run for the hills, when on our very first date, we were scheduled to go to the movies, and he arrived late to pick me up, reeked of marijuana, and went to sleep on me in the movie theater. Oh my gosh, it was the worst date ever! I literally ran out of the movie theater and told him to meet me by his car. Once he dropped me off, I flung the door open, jumped out, and ran to my house. I thought that I would never see that dude again.

The next morning, Mr. D apparently had an epiphany and showed up at my house with flowers and an apology for his appearance and behavior on our date. He really laid it on thick with his apology. Of course, a girl likes flowers. So yes, you guessed it. I gave Mr. D another chance.

We were dated for about three months. During our courtship, I honestly grew to like Mr. D. I even grew to love him. He was kind and considerate. Our first date seemed so far in the past at the time. He told me that he was working at his father's old dealership, that he was in school, and that he really wanted to break the cycle in his family by completing his education. I thought I was so lucky to have a dude who was courting me, super sweet, and not afraid to express his feelings for me—until my first reality check showed up.

One day, Mr. D called me out of the blue during the day, which I thought was strange. We rarely spoke during the day because of his "work" schedule. I answered the phone and heard loud music and a bunch of guys talking loudly in the background. I yelled, "Mr. D! Mr. D! Hello?" He didn't hear me. I hung up the phone because he had clearly butt-dialed me. But I was confused as to why I had heard a party in the background if he's supposed to be at work.

So the inquisitive spirit in me decided to call his mom. I know what you're thinking, *Oh, no, not his momma!* The truth is that his mother and I had a decent rapport with each other. I wanted to find out what was up. I called her. When she answered, she was all sweet and polite as usual. I started off with some small talk like, "How are you doing?" "Are you having a good day?" and "Don't you like the weather today?" And then I asked, "Is Mr. D at work today? He accidentally butt-dialed me, and I heard a bunch of noise in the background."

Mr. D's mother said, "What work? Mr. D did some work around the house for me, but that boy doesn't have a job."

Confused and troubled by this new information, I said, "Oh! Well maybe his job was getting in the way of his schoolwork."

She said, "School? Girl, that boy not in school!"

Now, I'm even more furious and looking crazy. I responded to his mom casually like she hadn't just told me that my boyfriend was a pathological liar. I thanked her for the information and told her that I'd call her later. Now flabbergasted by the blatant lies, I called Mr. D several times to get some answers. He finally picked up the phone.

I confronted Mr. D about this new information and tried to be calm about it. While we were on the phone, I said to him, "So how's your day going?"

He responded, "Good."

I said, "Oh, that's good to hear. You working hard today?"

He said, "Nah, I'm off today."

So now in my mind, I'm really livid because this guy was going to keep the lie going. I couldn't keep cool anymore and needed to spill the beans. I said, "Well, I spoke to your mom, and she told me you don't have a job and you aren't in school, so why are you lying to me?"

There was pure silence on the phone. After what seemed like an eternity, Mr. D cleared his throat and said, "Okay, it's true. I'm not working right now because I got let go at my job, and I've been breaking my neck to get another one."

I said, "Then why lie? And what about school?"

He said, "Truth is, I am enrolling in school again. I just haven't done it yet. I didn't tell you because I didn't want you to be ashamed of me." He continued, saying, "I feel like if I told you I wasn't as accomplished as you, I would just be letting you down."

My head dropped low. My heart was already invested

in this guy, and I instantly felt bad for him. I know. I know. I fell for the game. But at twenty years old and thinking that I had found the love of my life, I bit the bullet and carried on with the relationship, forgiving another red flag.

Later on, the lies continued. The more I sped to finish college and obtain my bachelor's degree, the more his drive and ambition decreased and then became nonexistent. That's right. Mr. D was turning into a bum. He began to show the extreme insecurities that were within him. He would start questioning me about my whereabouts because even he couldn't believe that I was still sticking with him after the lies. He began to get aggressive.

After two years and a web of lies, deceit, and laziness, the big breakup finally happened. I found out that he had cheated on me, and yes, I hate to admit it, but he also became abusive. I experienced domestic violence, an abortion, infidelity, and a ton of deceit all in one relationship. It was the end of the ordeal. The emotional wear and tear of that relationship opened the wound for more betrayal and infidelity. I was too young to recognize that Mr. D had created a trigger(s) for me. Later on down the line, I would continue this dating pattern.

The next love of my life was in 2014 when I met Mr. K. Mr. K was like a burning-hot fire, and I was the moth to his flame. Our relationship was very toxic but exhilarating. He had a way with words, he was *fine*, and he knew how to make me laugh. Some would say that he finessed me, that he was a charmer, and that he just downright intoxicated my spirit.

At the time, I was working at a prominent radio station in Chicago. Mr. K and I met through a mutual friend whom I worked with after Mr. K had asked about me at some event we both had been at. We exchanged numbers, and we went on our very first date on Valentine's Day in 2014. Mr. K was chivalrous and polite. He took me to a five-star restaurant and made me feel excited to be with him.

The chemistry between Mr. K and me was electrifying. I don't know what it was about him, but I lusted for him constantly and always wanted him around. It was like our energy was intoxicating.

We had been dating a few months. Then one night, we made plans for him to come to my house. We would just chill and enjoy our time together. Mr. K didn't show up. We had made plans to meet at my house by 8:00 p.m., and he was a no-show. I called him numerous times, but I couldn't get a hold of him.

I don't know what it is about a woman's nurturing heart that make us always want to fix men or go completely out of our way to prove that our love is real. But I instantly got concerned about his well-being. I kept thinking that something had happened to him. There was no way that he would just flake out on me without an explanation, unless something was wrong. Boy, was I wrong. Apparently, Mr. K had just decided to sit this night out and chill by himself, leaving me completely in the dark. I found this out on the following day. He called me to apologize and to tell me that once he had gotten home, he had just fallen sleep. Once again, my antennas went up, but to prevent an argument, I simply let it be known that he could've communicated something to me. And then, yes, you guessed it. I forgave him and wanted to move on. Not taking heed to the warnings, Mr. K and I continued to date for another two months.

One day, Mr. K called me in a panic. He claimed that his car had been repossessed, that he was behind by $500, and that he had no idea how he was going to get his car back. At the time, I was still building my own finances up, but I had come into some money, and I was feeling fake rich. Everything in me said, *Let him figure this out on his own.* But the young, naive, sweet, and giving spirit in me said, *You love him. You want to see him win.* So against my better judgment, I rushed to the bank, called in late for work, and told him that I'd loan him the money.

Mr. K promised that he would pay me in full in two weeks' time. He claimed that his siblings had received their income tax money. I'll admit that as I'm writing this and telling the world my past insecurities and young mistakes, I am immensely proud of my personal growth and willingness to forgive others' indiscretions, but man were these experiences learning curves.

Let's fast-forward to two weeks later. Mr. K began giving me the run around. Now granted, we were still dating and spending time with each other, but there was something tainted in our connection. Even before I learned to cultivate my spiritual powers and really tap into my intuition, I could always sense a shift when it was happening. But I didn't always make the necessary corrections when the shift occurred. Our relationship was no different. So when the time was up and I asked him for an update on my funds, he didn't oblige me. He started rambling and said that he was waiting on his siblings to pay him. Basically, he was saying that when he got it, I would get it. My spirit regretted this decision more and more, but I wasn't a petty woman. I was patient and still loving.

Let me further explain about the connection that Mr. K and I had. I have always been a hopeless-romantic type of lover who is attracted to a person's spirit, his sense of humor, and the unexplainable energy that I have with a love interest. I would say that Mr. K and I had that. Because of his courting, compliments, and sense of humor, he would make me feel as if I was the only girl in the world. I know that it's a cliché, but it's the honest truth. At least, it had been the energy that he had fed me with at the beginning of our journey.

As the relationship continued, he began to make me feel unappreciated and then disrespected. That wonderful sense of humor that I was so smitten with began to turn me off as I saw him use that same sense of humor to flirt with other women in front of me. Then there were more nights of him disappearing, and never keeping his word became more prevalent. It was apparent that I wasn't a priority in his eyes anymore.

Keep in my mind that this book isn't focused on lost love, pain, or betrayal. This is a book about self-love. It is a manifesto about how I grew to have unconditional love for myself and how you can do it too with your own affirmations.

So needless to say, Mr. K never gave me my money back. I experienced rejection and more deceit. I had a toxic acceptance of him, which enabled his behavior to change. I created a pattern that made it OK to go back and forth with someone whom I knew didn't deserve me. But I loved the thrill and chase of the destructive connection.

My biggest loss and latest love was in 2016 with Mr. DC. Mr. DC came into my life at a time of readiness and uncertainty. I was essentially ready to experience real love. I wanted everlasting love, but I was also uncertain of myself and the greatness that was embedded in my DNA, which I still needed to tap into. Nevertheless, Mr. DC played a pivotal and essential role in my life. We met online. We approached each other with optimism for love and getting to know each other.

Mr. DC was strong, intelligent, daring, funny, and ambitious. He had many aesthetic qualities that I admired and adored. Mr. DC and I moved fast in our courting stages. Within three weeks, we were in a relationship and practically living with each other. I had never felt or experienced such intense emotions for a person whom I was dating. I honestly created a codependent behavior with Mr. DC, that at the time, I wasn't aware of. But now that I've elevated my mind and done some rootwork on myself internally, I can say that it was true. I felt like I needed him in order to make myself feel good and wanted. In all actuality, I needed to pour that energy of love into myself.

After Mr. DC and I had expeditiously fallen in love, we tried to find ways to navigate through it. The difference was that I was *all in* while Mr. DC began to panic and withdraw his emotions from me. One day while I was on a business trip to Las Vegas, I remember feeling that Mr. DC wasn't very concerned with my well-being. I had grown accustomed to us calling and talking to each other throughout the day and every day. But once I had left on the business trip, communication had slowed down significantly. I called, and no one answered, or he would start sending me brief text responses, as if he didn't want to be bothered with me. I grew weary of racking my brain to figure out what was going on, especially because I was on a business trip. I had decided to stick a pin in my worrying thoughts until I returned home. I figured that maybe he wanted some alone time because I wasn't there.

After I had returned home and hadn't received a call from him to check to see if I had made it back safely, I became worried about his well-being. A couple of days went by, and I had still received no word from Mr. DC. Now granted, I wouldn't have panicked if the communication hadn't been so sporadic and almost nonexistent when I had been out of town. But now that I had returned and still hadn't heard from him, I grew nervous and feared that something had happened to him, due to his line of work. Mr. DC was a truck driver. So he often risked his life on the road.

Being the kind of girlfriend that I was, I went to find evidence that he was OK. I checked his social media, called him, texted him, and even had to go to the extreme of calling his workplace. I know that men are probably saying this is a no-no, but the truth is that I didn't care. It had been five days since I had spoken to him, and that was completely out of the norm. I kept thinking that there was no way he would just disappear without a trace, so something had to be wrong. I'll admit that I got creative with my phone call so that I didn't come across as a deranged girlfriend. I called his boss and disguised myself as a loan officer from the bank, who was calling to verify employment of one of their employees.

The call went like this, "Hello, sir. My name is Sarah, and I'm a loan officer from [unknown bank] calling to verify employment of Mr. DC. Is he still employed at your establishment?" And to my surprise, Mr. DC's boss confirmed employment and said that he was currently on the road as we spoke. I said to myself, *Oh, is he now?* I know all of this may sound crazy. Honestly, I wouldn't go through these great lengths anymore to figure out my relationships again.

After the call to his job, low and behold, Mr. DC arose from the grave. He called me instantly, but as excited as I was to hear from him, I quickly realized that I was being ghosted. So as excitement and relief entered my body, heartbreak and hurt feelings did as well. I couldn't for the life of me grasp how someone could say that he loved me, spend all day and almost every day with that person, and then ghost her.

A rush of anger overwhelmed my body while I was on the phone with him because I heard him trying to chastise me about calling his employment, but I never heard an apology for his disappearing acts. I instantly hung up the phone and literally fell into a ball of tears. I felt so hurt. Truthfully, I had never experienced this type of disappointment and abandonment until I met Mr. DC. I can honestly say that Mr. DC was my first real adult love.

Let me explain. My previous relationships had definitely been pivotal and important to me; however, I had felt like I was still in an adolescent stage of life. With Mr. DC, my love had grown. I had grown as an individual, especially spiritually. The love that I had experienced with him was pure and meaningful.

Mr. DC and I broke up after ghosting me for a few months. I realized he wasn't mature enough to have the relationship that I thought we had both agreed on. I was heartbroken and devastated that he wasn't in my life anymore. The breakup started to affect me physically. I had insomnia for three weeks. My spirit and light were disrupted. I was sad. I cried and harbored passive-aggressive behaviors, even in the workplace.

Have you ever heard of the term soul-tie? A soul-tie is when two individuals' souls and kindred spirits integrate with each other and create an unbreakable cycle and bond. By some crazy law of attraction according to the universe, soul-ties always find their way back to each other because they always yearn for each other's energy and eventually reconnect. I felt like Mr. DC and I had a soul-tie that wouldn't go away.

Mr. DC and I created a pattern of convenience and comfortability. After the ghosting debacle and five months of separation, Mr. DC and I reconnected. Yes, I was still in love. He had finally apologized for his actions, but his lack of commitment and maturity tainted our connection. Nevertheless, being the crusader of love that I was, I kept going and longing to fix our relationship.

Two years and a bucketful of tears and disappointments later, I was mentally and emotionally drained and need I say, broken by this relationship. It had gotten to the point that he didn't have the capability to love me the way that I needed him to, due to his own indiscretions. Officially walking away from the relationship began a necessary restoration of faith in myself and my energy. I had poured so much love into another person, it wasn't apparent to me that I had completely lost myself in the relationship. His needs had become my needs, his desires had become my desires, and his thoughts had become my thoughts. I felt had like a robot. And just like most robots, I needed to be seriously rebooted.

The journey of self-reflecting, self-love, and self-care began. I began to practice deep and constant meditation. Through my revelations, I also began to hold myself accountable for the parts that I had contributed to and allowed into those relationships that hadn't worked out. It was not a blame game anymore. I didn't want to become a victim or date assholes anymore. But I gained power within myself, and I was accountable. I faced some harsh realities about myself. I was acting in desperation to get the love that I was missing in myself.

Through my practices of healing, I began to re-center the love, energy, and devotion that I had poured into Mr. DC into myself. In the middle of the night when I began to reminisce on the energy that we had shared, I mentally replaced his name and face with my own. Let me elaborate. Instead of me thinking, *I love you, Mr. DC*, I thought, *I love you, Dana*. Instead of thinking, *I miss him*, I would think, *I miss me*, and so on and so on. I literally replaced those yearning serendipitous moments for him with healing and appreciation for myself.

In addition to chakra cleansing, I surrounded myself with rose quartz (love) crystals and sage my body and spirit frequently. I did this for myself six months to a year, just to feel like myself again. My logic behind this was, *How can I continuously pour love and support into someone else, but not myself?* It became painfully clear that I had indeed neglected my own thoughts and needs. A correction was necessary.

To add insult to injury almost a year later after our break up, Mr. DC called me to say 'thank you!' He told me the love I poured into him helped him to be a better father and a better person. That portion of the conversation I received very well, and it gave me a sense of validation, however the following words after his gratitude is what made me grateful for my healing journey. He then proceeded to tell me that he had a baby on the way and was getting married. I was in shock. I was in shock, because all during the relationship with me he told me he couldn't see himself being in a monogamous relationship with me, that monogamy just wasn't in the cards for him. We would also have conversations about having kids together and he would be terrified of having another child with a woman and it didn't work out, because of his past experiences. So as he boasted and raved about this whole new life he was starting with another woman, I felt myself drowning in the conversation and negative energy with him. You see he had triggered me and ignited those horrible emotions I had been trying to heal. So I needed to save myself and set the boundary and no longer torture myself, I immediately ended the conversation, hung up the phone and blocked him.

Being able to bounce back from a devastating loss or traumatic experience can be challenging but also liberating. My methods may not fix the current devastation that you may be in; however, I want you to challenge yourself to find a method that will remove hate, heartache, and disappointment and replace it with peace, patience, and unconditional love. The method can consist of the many things that I have already named in this book.

Throughout these specific events in my life, I'll admit that it created a trigger(s) for abandonment issues and a lack of trust and faith in healthy relationships. But I take these as lessons in navigating through uncharted territories of relationships. As I propel forward in life—specifically in dating—I am still unapologetic for the love I give, but I'm also cautious. The moment that adversity becomes present in my love life and triggers a bad or sensitive emotion, I digest it. I amplify my intuition to the problem and proceed with caution and boundaries but not fear. Boundaries set the tone for the things that you will and will not tolerate. They should be in place for every social interaction you have, including coworkers, family, friendships, and other relationships.

Set Boundaries and Stick to Them

The way that you interact, invite, and allow people into your life is based on the boundaries that you have in place for yourself. For instance, a boundary that I've set when it comes to dating involves deal breakers. These are my biggest deal breakers: a man who doesn't believe in God, a man who doesn't want children, or a man who doesn't believe in monogamy. I have these boundaries in place to guide me if I decide to pursue a romantic relationship with someone.

However, I've learned that boundaries can get misconstrued and lines can become blurred once that special chemical—serotonin (aka love)—gets involved. Whew! Love will cause your boundary lines to become smeared, pushed back, or even erased if you're not careful. By setting boundaries, you make conscientious decisions to protect yourself in any relationship that you're involved in. That goes for your friends, your boss, and especially your lover. It sets the tone for the way that you want to be treated and even more importantly, the way that you deserve to be treated.

The body naturally creates its own defense system to protect itself from outside viruses and bacteria. But what if setting boundaries is the natural defense mechanism to protect your heart? Now don't get me wrong. I'm not saying that you shouldn't be vulnerable or take risks. I'm saying that when you do these things, you should have a defense mechanism in place so that you will know your limits of tolerable behavior from a person. You also have to stick to these boundaries and make them your uncompromisable principles before a person has access to you. I want people to understand that this is a method that both men and women should follow so that they can receive the love and outcomes that they've been hoping for.

Setting boundaries and sticking to them can be difficult

and challenging. I sit back and wonder if I am being too harsh on the people that I think I want in my life or the men that I want to date, but the truth is that I tried the other option, which is either no boundaries at all or compromising them, and it never turned out right. I was going against the intuitive gifts that my ancestors had bestowed on me. I wasn't really being myself. In the end, I was getting hurt by people that I actually thought loved me. That's a far worse feeling than being proud that you stuck to your boundaries and stood in them with confidence. So the answer is no, you're not being too harsh. You're protecting yourself, and nothing is ever wrong with that.

Chapter 7
Having an Unbreakable Spirit

How to Navigate through
Negative Energies and Environments

As a TV producer, I spent years grinding and working my way up from the bottom of the totem pole. In the beginning of my career back in 2013, I started out by volunteering on sets. I connected with multiple independent filmmakers to learn the business and get my feet wet. In my journey to make it, I had to get creative to land a job in the mainstream television industry. I began going to visit several major studios and shows as an audience member. I networked and built rapport with people until I got my big break in 2016, to be a production assistant for a famous TV court show and judge. I was elated. It was my first big show, and I was hungry to learn everything that I could about the TV production industry.

I worked hard and built up my reputation with my executive producers and teammates. I landed a promotion after nine months of working there. Slowly but surely, I began to make a name for myself in the industry. Although getting a promotion was rewarding, the unnecessary coddling of my superiors' feelings and the work culture that perpetuated passive-aggressive behavior amongst the staff made the job tiresome and mentally draining.

When working in television, there's always the stigma of it's not what you know but who you know. This essentially means becoming chummy with a lot of your coworkers to fit in so that they will like you and vouch for your work, if that time ever comes. But the problem with this toxic mentality in the workforce is that you're always craving to be liked by your counterparts. You're too scared to rock the boat or go outside your comfort zone—not even a little bit—because you don't want to piss anyone off and not work in television again.

Honestly, the whole industry is an exhausting treadmill that you continue to run on, until you decide you want to get off. Television can be a rewarding experience, but it can also prey on your psyche if you're not strong enough to endure all of the games, manipulation, and lies that may be told about you throughout your career. I can't tell you how many times I was mentally tested during my television career. Some days, I did well. I was still excited to be working for a major network and TV show. But then other days, I felt like I was a joke. I felt that due to my nice demeanor and bubbly personality, my superiors would doubt my intelligence or just flat-out underestimate my abilities to excel in general. Those times were the gut punches that no one tells you can affect your confidence.

However, becoming more self-aware of the anguish that this job makes me feel and simply knowing my value as a worker have helped me prevail. I throw on a smile and my winning personality and continue to soar throughout the industry.

I honestly, want to start an initiative called '*Maintaining Your Mental Health, while Working in Television.*' The initiative would be geared to helping those cope with destructive behavior that tv professionals endure. It is a much-needed discussion that needs to happen frequently, but for right now I'll deal with one battle at a time.

After working at this TV show for several years, I was ready for a new challenge. I packed up all of my belongings and relocated to a new city and a new production. Now things got interesting. I learned how to navigate through a new city and job in no time. It was 2018, and I was well acclimated in my TV career. I began to get more jobs in the industry. Throughout my career, I have had great experiences while working there. Of course, the long and tiresome hours have been grueling on my mind and body, but I have grown accustomed to it.

Unfortunately while I was transitioning into this industry, I never had a mentor or an executive whom I could look up to, who was warm and willing to help me cultivate my producing skills. I learned and grew on my own, and I was very proud of myself. I did pretty well for myself while working with several networks: NBC, Warner Brothers, Comedy Central, VH1, Fox, and more. In 2020, I landed a job with another major network for another long-running TV show that millions had watched. During this time, I was elated because after going through an unfathomable event like a pandemic, new jobs equaled elevation for me—or at least I thought so.

I remember coming into the job with my high energy and allowing my presence to fill the room because I was happy to be working during a pressing time. In addition to this, I heard great things about this production and show, until it came under new management.

Have you ever seen a moth fly to a flame or flies to a light? The flies are so intrigued by the light that they grab hold of it because it's captivating. You'll see one fly to the light, and then another one follows, and then another follows. One after the other, they are attracted by the light. Before you know it, the light is covered by flies, and you don't even see the light anymore. It becomes a slew of disgusting flies covering what once was a beautiful light but now has been smothered by darkness.

There are going to be times when people may not understand your energy, presence, or gifts, but they know you're special. This threatens people. It could be the way you carry yourself, the sway in your hips, the power your voice holds when you speak, or that other people gravitate to you. Your mere existence and the power that they see you possessing will shake their whole world.

My new boss became one of those disgusting flies that I mentioned earlier. For whatever reason, this extremely insecure and threatened bully decided to make my TV experience a not-so-pleasant one. My new boss made it her business to purposely isolate me from team-building moments. She antagonized me through work emails and ultimately created a hostile work environment for me. Let me further explain, being a TV professional has its natural stresses: dealing with demands from the talent, being on point with logistics, and trying to create a healthy work balance for your duties. When you throw an unruly executive into the mix, things can get a little more complex and difficult.

I've heard rumors about horrid productions that force their crew to work twenty-four hours a day, with no breaks or food or the angry director on set who belittles and tells anyone or everyone to go fetch lunch. I will say that my environment wasn't that intense.

However, my old boss was calculated, manipulative, and miserable, which is a very bad combination for a person who's supposed to be your boss. I use that term very loosely because after a short time of working with her, I did not see her as any type of authoritative figure whatsoever. She wasn't the type of person to be brave or even woman enough to let you know what she was actually thinking about you. Rather, she hid her agendas and used her minions to do her dirty work. It's a cowardly approach to handling business, if I have to put a name to it.

At the start of my new season with this show, we hit the ground running with 110 percent effort and 0 percent support.

Working in the TV industry can be a lot of heavy work and a thankless job. Because of this, you can grow tired quickly. I often used to say that mental-health days were warranted in any demanding industry but unfortunately not always given. Truth be told, if more productions considered their workers' mental health, a lot of employees would be happier and would want to continue to thrive for their employers. When that's not an option, you have people who are simply coasting along for a check or until something better comes along.

While working at this specific production, the time finally came when I had had enough—enough of the passive-aggressive behavior and the poor directives and leadership that this person had inflicted on her staff. Specifically, I had become tired of this so-called boss trying to make me her personal objective to destroy my television career and everything that I had worked so hard to achieve. So I put my call to action in effect, and I filed a formal corporate complaint against my boss.

Here's where it really gets interesting. In my life or professional television career, I had never filed a complaint against an executive or boss before—*never.* I want to make sure that's clear so that people can understand how bad the environment had gotten for me and the staff.

After filing the complaint, things got worse. Soon the

network's intimidation tactics and retaliation came as a result of it.

Now picture this: a young black girl from Chicago, who had taught herself how to survive in this industry, going head-to-head with a network and its executive. It sounds crazy, right? I was in it, and it was crazy to me, but I was no longer going to stand for being mistreated or corporate bullied, when all I essentially wanted to do was work and excel at my career. So I fought them, and when I say fought, I'm referring to them to corporately. I had documented every unfair event, hostile email, excessive phone call, voice mail, text message, and any other disparaging act that was in place to intimidate or scare me away. Now granted, I'd never done anything like it before, but I was smart, efficient, and super-educated on employee rights.

I experienced discrimination, harassment, and a whole slew of other unethical behavior from this woman and her leadership. I gathered all of my documentation and presented it to the HR department. I just wanted me and other coworkers to be treated fairly and to not have to endure so much mental anguish from the likes of this person and her minions. My intentions were to create a safe space for people to just do their jobs, without petty retaliation, exclusion, and threats.

In the end, I realized that this action to stand up for myself was bigger than me and my experiences and that to have to speak out against any injustice in a workplace that condoned uncivilized behavior was unnecessary and unwarranted. After several months, the behavior that my boss had shown me died down but only momentarily. She even started treating the rest of her staff with some kind of decency. My whole goal was to hold a person in authority accountable. I wanted her to understand that becoming an executive meant that she had an obligation to treat her staff with some type of appreciation and consideration. She shouldn't discard them like trash or as if they weren't busting their butts every day to make a successful television show run.

While I was enduring these stormy events, I was forced to meditate and stay grounded more than I had ever before. I needed to make sure that I never stepped outside of my character or lashed out, even though my boss was instigating toxic behavior toward me. I did not waver. I stayed true to who I was. In fact, I elevated to an even higher vibration than I had before.

My point is that negative energies and situations are going to find their way to you; however, it all depends on how you deflect and resolve them. The whole purpose of elevating to your higher self is being able to control yourself in those situations.

Although I was excluded, discriminated against, and even harassed, I still was doing my job effectively. I was still pleased with the talent that I was booking, and I was on my A game, even though I had a miserable person trying to discredit me. When you believe in your higher self and have faith in your ancestors, you will overcome obstacles. I have a favorite saying that I have also had tattooed on my body: "C'est La Vie," which means, "That's life. No matter the circumstance, life will continue. You're either going to rise to the occasion or be eaten alive. I refused to be life's main course.

When I say navigating through negative energies, I'm not only referring to work stress but also relationship, dating, life, and hell, wondering-if-you-wanna-get-out-of-bed stress. With each stressful or uncomfortable moment that you encounter in life, you have to learn balance and stress management. I know dating stress alone used to leave me in negative spaces, especially if I really liked the guy and things didn't work out the way that I had expected. The disappointment, grief, and negative reactions I felt in those settings alone would have me in a whirlwind.

On a constant basis, I had to reassure myself of who I was and where I wanted to be. I needed to understand what I was representing every time I was personally attacked, my character was being diminished, and I was in relationships being undervalued and unappreciated. I had to become steadfast when overcoming obstacles and tribulations so that I could continue to evolve.

I want to elaborate on how to identify convoluted energies, which affect your mood and energy once you've encountered them. Have you ever walked into a room and stood next to a person who was having a bad day? Have you been able to pick up on a person's high or low vibrations just by conversing with that individual? That person's energies are just heavy. They are so heavy that negativity can even get transferred to you. You're left feeling angry or unsettled after having a negative conversation with a person.

These senses should become heightened the more you work on yourself and your self-love. You'll become more sensitive to the energies that you allow into your space and will learn to act accordingly. You'll become so aware of your spiritual environment that when the energy is not right, you'll know it.

Let's talk about discernment. Discernment is the perception that you'll receive when judgement is absent. Discernment is useful to obtain spiritual direction and understanding when there is no logic involved. When things occur in your life, they aren't so black and white, or you need to make a decision that is best for you, discernment can be a gift from God. On a daily basis, I pray for discernment. As you continue to navigate throughout this universe, discernment will be your saving grace. If you've ever heard of the saying, "Use your third eye," well baby, that's discernment or technically your sixth sense. As you proceed on your spiritual journey and elevate your powers, your discernment will have such a high vibration that you won't question certain things when it doesn't feel right to you. You'll know that it's not right for you and be content with that.

I typically use this saying or mantra when I am being tested, the universe is not on my side, and I'm experiencing some bad energies or situations: WWYHSD. I know that it looks like gibberish, right? I guarantee you that it is not. It means this: What would your higher self do? That's the question I typically ask myself when I feel myself unraveling or about to explode on a person who's not even worth the energy, like my previous boss whom I had the run-in with. I've learned to *not give my power away.* You cannot allow small people or energies to have a remote control over your emotions, your thoughts, or yourself in general.

To be frank, your higher or elevated self will always be the best version of you, which you currently are or aspire to be. If your higher self is successful, peaceful, and happy, that's who you are operating as so that you can stay on a higher vibration of enlightenment. You don't want to compromise that high vibration on a negative situation or energy that doesn't even serve a purpose for you.

On several occasions, I asked myself what would your higher self do because my higher self would always take the high road. She will always speak to people with love, understanding, and patience because that makes her feel good. My higher self will know how to remove itself from unwarranted or negative energies and maintain her peace or Zen *always.* So I'll pose the question to you now. What would your higher self do now that you have the tools to be better and can jumpstart a whole new life and energy for yourself?

Chapter 8

I Choose Me

On how many occasions have you suffered or become emotionally drained for the sake of someone else's feelings? What about suffering emotionally in order to keep the peace? I'm here to tell you to stop! Now don't get me wrong. You never want to create more chaos in your life; however, you cannot continue to be close mouthed or scared when you need to remove yourself from people, places, or circumstances that no longer serve you. I'm here to advocate for you to put yourself first without regrets.

In life, we are wired to nurture and take care of everyone else around us, even when it means putting other people's needs before our own. We sacrifice and bear it all but at what cost? Our mental security, our emotional support, and even our spiritual selves get drained, and we can't keep giving what we do not have.

Be Selfish

Yes, that's right. I'm telling you to be selfish for yourself and with your energy. I know that people may be thinking, *We despise selfish human beings.* At one point, I would have honestly agreed with you. People who are selfish and have no regard for other people's feelings are extremely frustrating to be around. But I've learned from the selfish people in my life to get happiness by any means necessary. I've decided to adapt to that way of thinking and make sure that I get my needs, wants, or desires met by any means necessary as well. That means cutting off people who don't fit into my spiritual circle.

I've been in this world for thirty-three years. In my thirty-third year, I have experienced the most transition. The number thirty-three is a divine numeral that stands for equilibrium and divine guidance. My thirty-third year allowed me to become selfish for myself. Let me explain further. I had to have some uncomfortable difficult conversations with people and cut off some friends. I had a few homegirls whom I felt were only focused on themselves and their needs. They would say to the hell with anyone else's.

Throughout my spiritual journey, I have learned to show a lot of my peers grace and understanding, for I know that they have been on their own spiritual journeys as well. But there comes a point when you need to choose yourself over them unapologetically. I had to be honest with myself and ask, *Am I getting my needs met in this friendship or relationship?* If the answer was no, I had a conversation with that friend. I was honest about what I was feeling.

True friend who values your friendship, your energy, and what you bring to the table in that friendship. That friend will be open to your concerns. He or she will want to explore and find out the reasons you're feeling that way. That friend will receive the conversation without malice or hostility. A person who is mature and aware of himself or herself will be okay with having that real conversation.

Unfortunately for me, those conversations with people whom I valued would always go south or result in an immature outcome, which my spirit was too tired to even deal with. The friendship would be dismantled. At one point, I was devastated when these friendships did not work out or strife was created. But now I think, *Good riddance.* It may sound harsh or even insensitive, but I'll tell you this: If you and a friend can't have a difficult conversation without things going south or becoming hostile, quickly run away from that relationship. Real friendships or relationships in general have some type of conflict. Conflict is inevitable, but the way you and that person handle conflict is the real testament of the friendship.

So do not be afraid of being selfish or allowing yourself to be open and candid about your true emotions and expectations with a person whom you are allowing into your energy. The only way to get what you want and need is to claim it and go after it. I am not saying that you should be rude or obnoxious while trying to get your needs met.

I am saying that you should start cherishing what you bring to the table more. You should cherish your energy and light. Remember that everything else about you is a privilege for anyone to be around. So I will say it again: Yes, you should be selfish and unapologetic about it.

In addition, be selfish with your time and space away from others when you need a spiritual refill. It's okay to remove yourself from others to ensure that you are becoming the best version of yourself. I am not saying that you should ghost people. One of the worst things you can do is disappear from a person's life without an explanation. I am saying that you need to have those difficult conversations with people in your life. It's okay to let them know, "I am not doing well spiritually and need your support [or space] in order to feel like myself again." These are all healthy conversations that you should have with the people who support you in any way.

Protect Your Peace

You can say that this is a self-explanatory statement. Let's take this up a notch and literally block anything and everything that does not contribute to your peaceful state. I cannot count the number of times I've been on a positive wavelength and then, "Boom!" a negative circumstance or person causes me to have a knee-jerk reaction that disrupts my peace. I cannot express how vital it is for you to be aware of your surroundings and their energies.

In life, there will be many circumstances that will dismantle or unravel your peace, but you have to be aware of them if you want to create a fortress of tranquility. Meditation, affirmations, and constantly speaking light into your life will perpetuate the high vibrations that you want to stay on. Changing your environment to meet the positive needs that you want to attract will be a big contributor to protecting your peace. People who surround themselves with like-minded individuals will nourish that peace and keep them on track.

No Self Doubt

I need you to eliminate your negative inner naysayer— the one that's always tells you what *not* to do because of fear. I recently started traveling by myself domestically and internationally. The amount of anxiety that I felt before stepping onto a plane by myself was unbearable. I began realizing that my inner naysayer was trying to take the reins of my life and tell me that I shouldn't or couldn't do the things that I had planned. However, with prayer and my daily affirmations, I filled myself with the confidence of knowing that I could do anything that I wanted to do.

I would be lying to you if *I* myself get in my own way and allow self-doubt to creep into my mind. I kid you not as I was getting my mindset together to write this book, I doubted myself. My inner naysayer told me, "Who are you to write a book?" At that moment, I'll admit I began to doubt myself, however when you're operating on pure unconditional love for yourself, you truly believe that anything is possible that you told yourself you can achieve. I did just that! I told myself that I am a woman who's trying to be a beacon of light to others, and they should want to hear what I have to say, because I am just like them.

Your inner naysayer is that small part of your consciousness that gets activated anytime you're about to do something that is unknown to you. Lock up that naysayer and throw away the key. Your inner naysayer serves no purpose other than causing you to walk in fear and self-doubt. It is literally the most toxic way of thinking when you are trying to elevate yourself spiritually and emotionally. The closer you get to stepping out in faith, the more your inner naysayer tells you not to do it and to stay comfortable and complacent with where you are. But the funny thing about life is that you are meant to be elevated, uplifted, and celebrated. Do not let fear prohibit you from getting all that life has to offer. Push yourself, be selfish, and move forward. I want you to choose *you* every single time.

Chapter 9

Spiritual Liberation

How dope would it be to have no spiritual inhibitions? To be free to feel, you must connect with and tap into all the power that you harness the moment that you remove mental blocks from your life. This is what it means to be spiritually liberated. You feel good. You feel elevated. But most importantly, you feel free.

I cannot express the amount of liberation I feel when I know that I've liberated myself from religious stipulations, titles, and identities. I completely and wholeheartedly allow God, the universe, and my ancestors to guide and show me the path that I am destined to be on in my human form. You see, meditation and enlightenment are gifts from God.

Long ago in Asian culture, people adapted to the idea and practices of Buddhism. They understood how to tap into their higher power, no matter what circumstances surrounded them. Spiritual liberation will always be present if you choose that path. Enlightenment originated in Western culture and spread through India, Southeast Asia, China, Korea, and Japan. Asian culture grasped the understanding of peace and how to harness its power a very long time ago. I feel that it's time to perpetuate that culture through our American one, specifically in African-American communities. There have been many instances when this type of talk becomes taboo or forbidden because of a lack of understanding. After conducting research on our ancestors from Egypt, Greece, Africa, and more, I don't know how our own practices of spiritual liberation got so lost in history.

Granted in Asian culture, Buddhism is a form of religion, but I'm removing the negative stigmas that are associated with belonging to or being forced inside a box called religion. I'm offering people spiritual elevation through the power of manifesting, paying homage to our ancestors, and meditation practices that heighten their spiritual senses. Let's be clear. Just because an individual doesn't identify with a religion does not mean that it's blasphemy or atheism. In my opinion, it means that the individual has surpassed the world's ideologies of what a Christian should be or look like. God is pure and open. I will even go as far as saying that God is fluid. God has no prohibitions or malice. He's just a pure entity who lives in all of us.

I distinctly remember that during an elevated meditation, I actually felt God's presence. I remember taking a solo trip out of the country to Panama. I purposely wanted to meditate in a different country and space so that I could tap into a different energy. I'm not sure why, but everything was more serene, still, and even clear. I remember that during my meditation, I saw bright colorful lights that were yellow, red and different hues of blue. My body began to warm up as tears rolled down my face. Now mind you, I was in my hotel room with the air-conditioning on and my eyes closed. I remember meditating on gratefulness.

I know that some readers may not believe this, but truthfully, I felt the presence of God in those colorful lights and the warmth on my skin. I felt safe, protected, and loved. I was in another country by myself, but I felt the most protected that I have in a while, on that trip right after my meditation. So I also want to say to others that meditation can be what you want it to be: an escape, a release, a safe haven, redemption, or even your godly portal to another dimension—if you will it so. Becoming spiritually liberated gives you no limits or rules because you're creating your own spiritual sanctuary.

I want to share the seven factors and levels of awakening, according to a group of southeastern monks, which properly communicate the levels of spiritual liberation and ultimately, peace and tranquility in your everyday life. You can achieve these.

The Seven Levels of Awakening

Level 1: Mindfulness

You may have ever been told the phrase, "Be mindful," which simply means to be completely aware of your reality. Too many times people, including myself, falter when trying to be mindful of their intentions, words, and even actions. Becoming more aware of your reality and circumstances can absolutely be a powerful thing. You see, when you're aware of your reality, it means that you're becoming more self-aware—of what you need to work on within yourself. It means that you can harness the power that will change your reality if you seek evolution and elevation in your life.

Level 2: Investigation

This is the power to explore and investigate the nature of your reality. After becoming self-aware of your surroundings, circumstances, and you as an individual, you must investigate this newfound power of wakefulness. Ask yourself questions. Question the reason that you may be feeling or not feeling a certain way. Explore your newfound emotions and mental capacity, which knows the way that you deal with trauma, stress, or happiness. In this level, I'm asking you to listen to yourself and then be intentional about giving yourself what you need in your newfound discoveries.

Level 3: Energy

Throughout this book, I've been stressing how imperative energies are. But what's most important is having the right energy around and *in* you as you navigate throughout this universe. In this level, you are declaring the determination and effort that you want to achieve so that you can obtain the energy you want to be around.

I have removed myself from a lot of people and situations where the energy was no longer meshing well with mine. It's called peace. Peace is investigating those feelings that you have begun to listen to. Intentionally acknowledge the things that do not fit into your spirit anymore. Once you remove that energy, you feel at ease and serene. I'm here to tell you that it is perfectly OK to isolate yourself from things that no longer serve you or energy that doesn't make you feel good anymore.

Level 4: Joy

It's a huge triumphant step to accomplish in an uncharted journey: having joy. Joy is the warmth you feel when you step outside and into the sun after you've been in darkness for a significant length of time. As a human moving throughout this world in so many unknown circumstances, being surrounded by a jovial presence is what I call winning. If you're filled with joy and happiness when you do the simplest and most minuscule things, consider yourself lucky and give yourself a gigantic pat on the back because becoming spiritually grounded and liberated is about the journey of achieving joy and maintaining it.

Level 5: Tranquility

Here we find a big contributing factor in maintaining that joy we've worked so hard to get. A tranquil nature will allow you to see the bigger picture in any situation and access that situation according to the level of serenity you want to maintain. It means that we should *pick our battles wisely.* Once you've done the work, lay down the ground rules and set the tone for what you will and will not allow in to disturb your peace. Then tranquility will come easily.

Level 6: Concentration

A calm state of mind and clear awareness are required on a journey to being spiritually liberated and awake. Throughout these other levels, you are meant to explore, discover, and listen to yourself so that the self-awareness needed to begin your spiritual elevation can be created. However, it takes a great deal of concentration to uphold this new, high vibrational energy, which you will be on once you've done the work. Staying steadfast regarding your mental and spiritual safety should always be a priority and goal that you want to achieve. It requires concentration and having clear thoughts so that you will know as well as understand what it looks like.

Level 7: Equanimity

This last but pivotal step is where you accept reality as it is and not as you think it should be or can change it to when things are out of your control. Pure, spiritual liberation is accepting the fact that there's going to be trials and tribulations in everyone's journey. The only thing that you can control in those times of crisis is yourself and your own well-being. Elevating to the height of equanimity means that you will no longer force situations, circumstances, or relationships that do not serve you or fit you and your journey. You are completely accepting the fact that peace becomes you and you are in control of all things *you*.

I want you to be able to enjoy your journey to spiritual liberation and embrace the struggles, trauma, and heartache because it does not belong to you. Embrace it with the intention of releasing it because it does not serve you. I know some may say it's not that easy to just forget a person's past or troubling experiences, and I wholeheartedly agree with you. I have gone through trauma myself. However, when I say it doesn't serve you, I mean that it does not define you, and you should not succumb to those experiences. Instead, you are learning from and releasing them because in the end, it does not belong to you. Insecurity, fear, trauma, alcoholism, financial hardship, self-hate, and doubt—release them! I promise that once the burdens of your past and the scars that they have left are released, you will find a new you. I absolutely can't wait to see what you will be then.

Notes:

Thomas McDaniels," 7 Ways Dynamic Quotes Inspire Our Lives" *Farnsworth's Classical English Rhetoric* (David R. Godine, Publisher; First Edition (November 15, 2010)

Wikipedia, *Shaw, Carl A. (2014), Satyric Play: The Evolution of Greek Comedy and Satyr Drama, Oxford, England: Oxford University Press, ISBN 978-0-19-995094-2, pg 5*

Printed in the United States
by Baker & Taylor Publisher Services